The Husband 101 Workbook

AN INTERACTIVE CO-ED STUDY GUIDE

The Husband 101 Workbook

AN INTERACTIVE CO-ED STUDY GUIDE

A'NDREA J. WILSON

Divine
Garden
Press

WWW.DIVINEGARDENPRESS.COM

Published by Divine Garden Press
PO Box 371
Soperton, GA 30457
www.divinegardenpress.com

ISBN-13: 978-0615716114
ISBN-10: 0615716113
Library of Congress Control Number: 2012952577

Cover Photograph: © Niderlander|Dreamstime.com

Cover Design: A'ndrea J. Wilson

Table of Contents

Letter from the Author

Dear Reader/Husband 101 Student,

The Husband 101 Workbook was created to allow the reader to slow down and retain the lessons from the novel, Husband 101. After I released the first novel in the series, Wife 101, it became apparent that readers not only wanted to enjoy the entertainment quality of the book, but also integrate the biblical and life lessons of the main character with their own lives. The Wife 101 Workbook was produced to offer readers a tool for self-growth and development. In the same manner, The Husband 101 Workbook aims to provide a similar benefit for readers of Husband 101.

The one change that I have made to The Husband 101 Workbook that does not appear in The Wife 101 Workbook is the co-ed focus. Because the novel is for everyone (both men and women), I wanted the workbook to also be relevant for both genders. Most questions can be answered by both genders. However, some questions contain bolded "men" and "women" labels. These labels are designed to indicate, based on your gender, which question is more applicable to you. As you proceed through the workbook, feel free to read all of the questions and answer the ones that are most appropriate for you and your situation.

The Husband 101 Workbook is an opportunity to reflect on the 31 lessons of the book, the 13 verses in I Corinthians 13, and the 13 classes that make up Husband 101. If you have not already read the novel, I highly recommended either reading the novel prior to completing the workbook or simultaneous to completing the workbook. The lessons in the workbook follow along with the lessons in the novel and have mirroring titles for easy use. Use this workbook to build a stronger relationship with God and your spouse/significant other. Take your time as you answer workbook questions and seek God for understanding in your life.

The Husband 101 workbook is a great tool for groups, marriage ministries, book clubs, or individual study. I would love to hear from you about how this workbook is blessing you and your group. Correspondence can be emailed to me at drajwilson@gmail.com or via the contact form on www.andreawilsononline.com or www.husband101.com.

Happy Reading & Journaling!

A'ndrea J. Wilson, Ph.D.

Lesson 1: Temptation Is Everywhere

Be well balanced (temperate, sober of mind), be vigilant and cautious at all times; for that enemy of yours, the devil, roams around like a lion roaring [in fierce hunger], seeking someone to seize upon and devour. (I Peter 5:8)

Eric opens the book discussing temptation and how it seeks to keep men from being whom they desire to be.

Men: Can you relate to the first paragraph of lesson one? How has temptation impacted your life?

Women: Are you aware of the temptations that the man in your life struggles to overcome? List them.

_____

_____

_____

_____

_____

Are there things or people that you feel you cannot tell your spouse/significant other about? Why?

_____

_____

_____

_____

_____

_____

_____

_____

Read I Peter 5:8. Write down your thoughts and/or feelings about this verse.

_____

_____

_____

_____

_____

_____

_____

_____

_____

_____

_____

_____

_____

_____

_____

_____

_____

_____

_____

_____

_____

_____

_____

Lesson 2: One Poor Choice Can Lead To A Lifetime Of Pain

Should your offspring be dispersed abroad as water brooks in the streets? [Confine yourself to your own wife] let your children be for you alone, and not the children of strangers with you.

(Proverbs 5:16-17)

Lesson two reveals the existing tension between Eric's wife and the mother of his child.

Men: Does a past relationship have an impact on your current relationship? How do you manage the two?

Women: How do you think men should handle past relationships when children are involved?

_____

_____

_____

_____

_____

During the second lesson, we also find out that Eric's ex-girlfriend is able to withhold his child from him because he does not have legal custody. What are your thoughts/feelings about the custody rights of fathers?

_____

_____

_____

_____

_____

_____

_____

Amber offers to provide Eric with legal help to deal with his custody issues, but Eric refuses it. Why do you think Eric rejects his wife's assistance?

_____

_____

_____

_____

_____

Read Proverbs 5:16-17. Discuss your thoughts about what these verses mean.

_____

_____

_____

_____

_____

_____

_____

_____

_____

_____

_____

_____

_____

Lesson 3: Know When It's Time To Leave & Cleave

Therefore a man shall leave his father and his mother and shall become untied and cleave to his wife, and they shall become one flesh. (Genesis 2:24)

In lesson three, readers get to know Eric's parents and his brother. His relationship with his family has a big influence on his decisions and behaviors. How does your relationship with your family impact who you are and how you behave? Are there habits or traditions that you practice that come from your family of origin?

_____

_____

_____

_____

_____

_____

_____

_____

Amber calls Eric a momma's boy when he goes to his parent's house for dinner instead of having Sunday dinner with her. Can you relate to Eric's relationship with his mother? Do you feel that the nature of a person's relationship with their family should change once they become married?

_____

_____

_____

_____

Read Genesis 2:24. Write down your thoughts and feelings about this verse.

_____

_____

_____

_____

_____

_____

_____

_____

_____

_____

_____

_____

_____

_____

_____

_____

_____

_____

_____

_____

_____

_____

Lesson 4: Sacrifice Is A Consequence Of Love

Husbands, love your wives, as Christ loved the church and gave Himself up for her...Even so husbands should love their wives as [being in a sense] their own bodies. He who loves his own wife loves himself. For no man ever hated his own flesh, but nourishes and carefully protects and cherishes it, as Christ does the church. (Ephesians 5:25, 28-29)

"Sometimes as men, we think we've got it all figured out. We think we know what we're doing, what God would have us to do. We've got a plan, we're working our plan, and we are so sure that our plan is what we have to do, what we need to do. Then God speaks to us and says, 'No, take a different path. Go a different way. This is not the way.' And what do we do? We fight it. We resist. We can't let go of our plans. We have worked too hard, strategized too much, gotten so caught up in our determination to make it work that we are unwilling to heed to God's voice. So we continue on down the wrong path. Our pride won't let us turn back. And one day, we wake up, and our whole lives are in shambles."

During the first Husband 101 class, Martin admits to his own struggle at times with changing his plans when God shows him a different way.

Men: How often do you find yourself struggling with obedience to God when His plans are different from your own? Discuss why this challenges you or why it is so hard to change once you already have a set plan.

Women: Do you find it difficult to get your spouse/significant other to change directions? How do you deal with a stubborn partner?

_____

_____

_____

_____

_____

_____

_____

_____

"I am passing out a piece of paper that has one question on it: Why do I love my wife? If you are not married, you can change the word to girlfriend or fiancé. If you're not in a relationship, think about the last serious relationship you had with someone that you loved. Take a few moments and write down your answer."

Men: The men in the Husband 101 class were asked to write down why they love their wives or girlfriends. Take a few minutes to answer this question for yourself.

Women: Why do you think your husband/boyfriend loves you? Why should they love you?

_____

_____

_____

_____

_____

_____

_____

_____

_____

_____

_____

_____

_____

_____

_____

_____

_____

Lesson 5: Be Able To Recognize The Signs

A wise man suspects danger and cautiously avoids evil, but the fool bears himself insolently and [presumptuously] confident. (Proverbs 14:16)

Eric feels that he must hide his business relationship with a female client from his wife due to the fear of how his wife may react. How do you feel about his choice? How would you recommend he deal with the situation?

_____

_____

_____

_____

_____

_____

_____

_____

_____

Eric ends up having a conversation with his female client and shares a few things with her about his wife.

Men: Do you have female friends that you talk to about your marriage/relationship? Why or why not? How can this impact your relationship with your significant other?

Women: How do you feel about the man in your life discussing your relationship with others? Does it matter if the person they are sharing details with is a male versus a female? Why?

_____

_____

_____

_____

_____

_____

_____

_____

_____

_____

_____

_____

_____

_____

_____

_____

Read Proverbs 14:16. Write down your thoughts about the meaning of this verse and how it applies to your life.

_____

_____

_____

_____

_____

_____

_____

_____

Lesson 6: Everything Means Nothing Without Love

And if I have prophetic powers (the gift of interpreting the divine will and purpose), and understand all the secret truths and mysteries and possess all knowledge, and if I have [sufficient] faith so that I can remove mountains, but have not love (God's love in me) I am nothing. (I Corinthians 13:2)

"Some of you may be just noise makers in your home. You are talking, saying all the right things, but because of the absence of God's love, it all sounds like Charlie Brown's teacher. 'Wan-wan-wan wan-wan.' Your words fall on deaf ears. You're wondering why no one listens when you speak, why no one follows your directions, why no one seems to care what you have to say. Your words are just noise. The love is missing."

During the second class, Martin discusses the first three verses of I Corinthians 13. Verse one deals with speaking without love. Read this verse, as well as Martin's explanation of it, and write down your thoughts or experiences about speaking without the presence of love.

_____

_____

_____

_____

_____

"Intelligence minus love might be the problem for some of you. You might be a brilliant person, see and understand things that no one else does, but you can't figure out why no one gives you any credit, why no one promotes you, why no one even likes you. You're intelligent, you're wise, but without love, you're nothing."

Martine explains verse two as having knowledge and wisdom without love. Read this verse and write down your thoughts or experiences related to having knowledge/wisdom without the presence of love.

_____

_____

_____

_____

_____

"Love, it takes love, and this might be your issue. You give and you give. You try to buy people with gifts. You think that if you give all of your time or sacrifice your safety that people will respect you, adore you. You will spend every dollar you make trying to wine and dine your wife. She has all of the newest and most expensive jewelry, lavish cars and houses, everything she could ever want, but your love because God's love is not in you. To her, you've done nothing at all. She still wants a divorce, and she still doesn't appreciate or respect you. On her way out the door she tells you, 'Get your checkbook ready, Mister. I want half.' "

Martin discusses verse three as giving without having love. Read verse three and write down your thoughts and experiences about giving without the presence of love.

_____

_____

_____

_____

_____

"I'm going to give you all another assignment. Take out your notebooks and pens if you don't already have them out. On a sheet of paper, I want you to write down the things that you are most proud of. Write down your accomplishments, your hopes, and dreams. What is it that you are working towards? What is it that you are really good at? What's your talent or skill? Take a few minutes to write a list of these things...Now, tear the piece of paper out of your notebook and take another piece of paper from your notebook, leave it in the notebook, but copy the list you have onto that new piece of paper...Okay the piece of paper that you have torn out, I want you to rip it up. Tear it into pieces and come up to the front and throw the pieces away into the trash can up here...The next thing I want you to do is take the remaining list and in big letters covering the entire page, write the letters L-O-V-E...I know it had to hurt some of you when you had to rip up the paper with the things that were important to you, but that's what happens without love. Your plans, hopes, and dreams are nothing. All that you think matters, doesn't. But when you covered what was important with love, now your plans, hopes, and dreams are something. Now they matter. Now they remain."

Create a list of your own accomplishments and goals on the lines below. Find another sheet of paper and copy the list. Rip up the list as Martin directed the class to do and throw it away. Then write the word LOVE over the list below. Finally, write down your emotions and thoughts about your experience doing this activity.

_____

_____

_____

_____

_____

_____

_____

_____

_____

_____

_____

_____

_____

_____

_____

_____

_____

_____

_____

_____

_____

Lesson 7: When It Sounds Too Good To Be True . . .

The simpleton believes every word he hears, but the prudent man looks and considers well where he is going. (Proverbs 14:15)

In lesson seven, Eric's ex-girlfriend Lena shows up at his door, upset about having to go court for shared custody of their daughter. Why do you think parents who are no longer together struggle with sharing custody of the children? Do you agree with Eric's decision to take the matter to court? Why or why not?

_____

_____

_____

_____

_____

Eric's client Jay offers him an opportunity that he finds difficult to turn down. Unfortunately, the opportunity comes with a string. What are your thoughts about this scene and Eric's response to her proposition? How would you have handled the situation if you were in Eric's shoes?

_____

_____

_____

_____

_____

_____

_____

Read Proverbs 14:15. Write down your thoughts and feelings about the meaning of this verse and how it applies to your own life.

_____

_____

_____

_____

_____

_____

_____

_____

_____

_____

_____

_____

_____

_____

_____

_____

_____

_____

_____

_____

_____

_____

_____

Lesson 8: Hang In There!

Love endures long and is patient and kind; love never is envious nor boils over with jealousy, is not boastful or vainglorious, does not display itself haughtily. (I Corinthians 13:4)

Read I Corinthians 13:4, as well as Martin's discussion of this verse. He breaks down the meanings of key words in this verse. Take the time to think about the definition of each word and write down how easy or hard it is for you to express each aspect of love in your relationship and why.

ENDURES LONG

_____
_____
_____
_____
_____
_____
_____
_____
_____

PATIENT

_____
_____
_____

KIND

NEVER ENVIOUS/JEALOUS

NOT BOASTFUL/VAINGLORIOUS

_____

_____

_____

_____

_____

_____

_____

_____

_____

DOES NOT DISPLAY ITSELF HAUGHTILY

_____

_____

_____

_____

_____

_____

_____

_____

_____

_____

_____

Lesson 9: What Goes Up Must Come Down

Rejoice not when your enemy falls, and let not your heart be glad when he stumbles or is overthrown. (Proverbs 24:17)

Eric feels insecure about his wife's relationship with her ex-fiancé and expresses his concern.

Men: How do you deal with other men communicating with your spouse/significant other? Do you tend to feel jealous or insecure? Are you afraid of your partner cheating on you with another man?

Women: Is your spouse/boyfriend jealous of your exes or other men in your life? How would you/do you handle his concerns about other men?

_____

_____

_____

_____

_____

Eric makes a statement to his mother that he feels like he has fifty pounds of weight on his shoulders. Do you ever feel overwhelmed and weighed down by the issue of life? How do you de-stress or cope?

_____

_____

_____

_____

_____

Nelson and his friends attempt to give Eric relationship advice. What are your thoughts about these men and the way they view Eric? Do you think Eric responded to them in an appropriate manner? Are there people like these men in your life who offer similar advice? How do you respond to them?

_____
_____
_____
_____
_____
_____
_____
_____

Read Proverbs 24:17. Write down your thoughts and feelings about this verse.

_____
_____
_____
_____
_____
_____
_____
_____
_____
_____
_____
_____

Lesson 10: Stop Acting Like A Clown

It is not conceited (arrogant and inflated with pride); it is not rude (unmannerly) and does not act unbecomingly. Love (God's love in us) does not insist on its own rights or seeking its own way, for it is not self-seeking; it is not touchy or fretful or resentful; it takes no account of the evil done to it [it pays no attention to a suffered wrong]. (I Corinthians 13:5)

"The second aspect of the verse says that love is not rude and doesn't act unbecomingly. Unbecomingly is a nice and proper way to say acting like a fool, or as I call it, a clown. If you are running around the house screaming at everyone, if you are cutting your wife down in front of folks or making sly comments to her family and friends, if you are racing up to her job causing a scene in the parking lot, and if you are calling people in her cell phone contact list trying to find out who she is talking to, you are out of order and not from a place of love."

Read I Corinthians 13:5. Have you ever found yourself "acting like a clown" toward someone you love? Write down your thoughts, feelings, or experiences, and how this part of verse five relates to you.

_____

_____

_____

_____

_____

"But seriously, how many of us have to have our way? Men, we can be harsh like that. It's either our way or the highway. If she doesn't want to do things the way we want or like, she has to go, or we're leaving. We feel we can find another woman who will give us what we want. That's not love, y'all. Love is not self-seeking, which means if I love you, I am not going to force my way upon you."

Is your behavior toward your partner self-seeking? Write down your thoughts, feelings, or experiences related to self-seeking behavior and how it negatively impacts love.

_____

_____

_____

_____

_____

"Love is not touchy, fretful, or resentful. In laymen's terms, love is not sensitive, easily or constantly offended, or highly irritable. Some of you all, everything your wife says gets on your nerves. Some men just stay mad, just stay annoyed. Come on! We can't have good relationships with the people we care most about if we always have an attitude about something...God separates our sins, our wrongs from us, and says He remembers them no more. It's like it never happened. He wants us to do the same. Whatever your wife, your girlfriend, or anyone else that you love did to you, count it as forgotten. Burn the records. It's over. That's how you strengthen your love in a relationship; you forgive and forget."

Read Martin's lecture related to the last part of verse five. Write you're your thoughts, feelings, or experiences about forgiveness, offensiveness, and resentment in your relationship.

_____

_____

_____

_____

_____

_____

_____

_____

_____

_____

Lesson 11: Success Has A Price

The earnings of the righteous (the upright, in right standing with God) lead to life, but the profit of the wicked leads to further sin. (Proverbs 10:16)

In lesson eleven, Eric decides to go to the party with Jay and compromises his vows by moving his wedding ring from his ring finger to his middle finger? Do you agree with his decision? Why or why not?

_____

_____

_____

_____

_____

Jay expresses her romantic interest in Eric. Once she does so, should Eric continue to work with her? Have you ever been in a similar situation? If so, how did you manage it?

_____

_____

_____

_____

_____

Eric finds himself being dishonest to his wife about his activities with his client? How does dishonesty in a relationship/marriage negatively impact the bond between the couple?

_____
_____
_____
_____
_____
_____
_____
_____
_____

Read Proverbs 10:16. Write down your thoughts and feelings about this verse.

_____
_____
_____
_____
_____
_____
_____
_____
_____
_____
_____
_____
_____
_____
_____
_____

Lesson 12: Love Is The Truth

It does not rejoice at injustice and unrighteousness, but rejoices when right and truth prevail.

(I Corinthians 13:6)

"There are a lot of us who rationalize our wrong doing, using the excuse of love. 'I love my wife, so that's why I lie to her about my drinking, my gambling, or that other woman.' Or how about, 'What my wife doesn't know won't hurt her.' And we cannot leave out this one, 'I think I'm in love with this other woman, and if loving her is wrong, I don't want to be right.' Let's be real, family. This is not love; it's selfishness, and it's sin. Love rejoices with the truth. If there is something you are deceiving yourself or your woman about, it's time to come clean."

Eric tells a lie and omits the truth to protect himself and possibly even his wife's feelings. Based on Martin's discussion of love being truthful, what are your thoughts about Eric's lying and withholding the truth? Do you ever lie to your spouse/mate? Why?

_____

_____

_____

_____

_____

_____

_____

_____

_____

_____

_____

_____

_____

_____

Read I Corinthians 13:6. Write down your thoughts and feelings about this verse.

_____

_____

_____

_____

_____

_____

_____

_____

_____

_____

_____

_____

_____

_____

_____

_____

_____

_____

Lesson 13: Confession Is Good For The Soul

A [consistently] righteous man hates lying and deceit, but a wicked man is loathsome [his very breath spreads pollution] and he comes [surely] to shame. (Proverbs 13:5)

Eric has experienced some setbacks in his life that have prevented him from being where he feels he should be. Can you relate? Do you ever struggle with feelings of being "behind" in life or unable to reach your goals? Have you ever felt that you have to give up your happiness or goals for the sake of others? Write down these thoughts, feelings, or experiences.

_____

_____

_____

_____

_____

_____

_____

_____

_____

_____

Eric attempts to tell Amber about his client, but finds himself unable to say the words? Are you good at communicating your feelings or do you struggle with telling people your inner emotions? How can you improve your communication skills with your spouse/significant other?

_____

_____

_____

_____

_____

_____

_____

_____

_____

_____

Eric realizes that Amber and Jay have a lot in common which complicates his relationship with his client Jay. Are you attracted to certain qualities in the opposite sex? How can awareness of what attracts you help you avoid unnecessary temptation?

_____

_____

_____

_____

_____

_____

_____

_____

_____

_____

Read Proverbs 13:5. Write down your thoughts and feelings about this verse and how it applies to your life.

_____

_____

_____

Lesson 14: Love Can Handle It

Love bears up under anything and everything that comes, is ever ready to believe the best of every person, its hopes are fadeless under all circumstances, and it endures everything [without weakening]. (I Corinthians 13:7)

"But I'm here today to tell you that it's time to believe again. I'm not saying that people won't hurt you because many will. But love says that even if you hurt me, I still believe the best in you. I still know that you're a child of God and that He created you to be better than this, and if you only reconnect with His love, you will return to being your best again. Believe in your wives; believe in your girlfriends and fiancés. Stop thinking so negatively. Maybe the reason they keep disappointing you and hurting you is because you believe that's what's going to happen anyway. Faith has the power to move mountains, but if our faith or belief is negative, it also has the ability to move things in the opposite direction."

Read I Corinthians 13:7, as well as lesson fourteen in your Husband 101 book. Write down your thoughts and feelings about this verse and how it reflects what God wants for marriage. Especially consider the following questions: Are you willing to bear any and all things for the sake of love? Do you believe the best of your spouse/significant other? Do you still have hope when all hope should be lost? Will your love endure without weakening? If you find that your love for your spouse is less than what is describe in verse seven, how can your relationship with God fill in the gaps in your loving?

_____

_____

_____

_____

_____

_____

Lesson 15: You're No Better Than The Rest

Many a man proclaims his own loving-kindness and goodness, but a faithful man who can find?
(Proverbs 20:6)

Eric's family suffers a major blow with the exposure of Eric's father's past affair. What are your thoughts about lesson fifteen? Can you relate to Eric, Nessy, or Dwayne? What are the consequences of an affair on the people involved and their families?

_____

_____

_____

_____

_____

_____

_____

_____

_____

Read Proverbs 20:6. Write down your thoughts about this verse and how it applies to you.

_____

_____

_____

Lesson 16: Love Stays

Love never fails [never fades out or becomes obsolete or comes to an end]. As for prophesy (the gift of interpreting the divine will and purpose), it will be fulfilled and pass away; as for tongues, they will be destroyed and cease; as for knowledge, it will pass away [it will lose its value and be superseded by truth]. (I Corinthians 13:8)

"Everything in this world will eventually fail. Our government fails, our physical structures fail, relationships fail, and even nature fails, but love, God's love, never fails. There is no end to it, it never fades, and it never becomes outdated or unnecessary. With God's love working and living in us, we are also able to express that kind of love towards others, including our women. We are able to love them in a manner that is endless and timeless. People are often awed when they hear of marriages that have lasted fifty or more years. Why? Because we see love as a temporary state, as something that fades away over time. It is difficult for us to imagine spending half of a century with the same person, but God's love in us can last to the end of time and beyond."

Read I Corinthians 13:8 and lesson sixteen of the Husband 101 book. Write down your thoughts and feelings about this verse and Martin's lecture on it.

_____

_____

_____

_____

_____

_____

_____

_____

_____

The men in the class break out into singing upon the mention of Heatwave's *Always and Forever*. If you don't know all of the words to this song, look them up online. How is this song relevant to I Corinthians 13:8?

_____

_____

_____

_____

_____

_____

_____

_____

_____

_____

_____

_____

_____

_____

_____

_____

_____

_____

_____

_____

_____

_____

Lesson 17: The Pot Calling The Kettle Black

He who has no rule over his own spirit is like a city that is broken down and without walls.

(Proverbs 25:28)

Jay continues to try to entice Eric through career advancement opportunities. What are your thoughts about Jay and her determination to tempt a married man?

Men: Do you agree with the manner that Eric responds to Jay or would you respond differently?

Women: How would you like your spouse/boyfriend to respond to a woman like Jay?

_____

_____

_____

_____

_____

Eric confronts his father about the affair. Do you think he has a right to feel resentful toward his father? Does his father owe him an explanation?

_____

_____

_____

_____

_____

Read the last paragraph of lesson seventeen. Write down your thoughts or feelings about Eric's epiphany about why men cheat.

_____

_____

_____

_____

_____

_____

_____

_____

_____

Read Proverbs 25:28. Write down your thoughts and feelings about this verse and how it applies to you.

_____

_____

_____

_____

_____

_____

_____

_____

_____

Lesson 18: No More Excuses

But when the complete and perfect (total) comes, the incomplete and imperfect will vanish away (become antiquated, void, and superseded). (I Corinthians 13:10)

"Don't use that tired old excuse, 'God's still working on me.' The work is already done. All you've got to do is empty yourself of you and let Him reign as Lord over your life, and He is able to demonstrate His perfect love through you towards your wife who is also His bride. Yes, on your own you are incomplete, imperfect, destined to fail, but with God in you and working through you, you are a man and a husband that is able to love your wife as Christ loved the church and gave His life for it. You can, even right now, love as God loves because He is in you, giving you the power and ability to be complete in your loving. You just have to believe it, receive it, and move out of His way. Surrender to His love, brothers. No more excuses."

Read I Corinthians 13:10 and lesson eighteen. Write down your thoughts and feelings about this verse and Martin's explanation of it.

_____

_____

_____

_____

_____

_____

_____

_____

_____

_____

_____

_____

_____

_____

Eric and Amber enjoy an evening of friendship and fun following the Husband 101 class in lesson eighteen. Over time, many couples stop doing things together that are pleasurable which often has a negative impact on their relationships. How often do you have fun with your spouse/significant other? What activities do you both enjoy? How can you add more enjoyable activities with your mate to your schedule?

_____

_____

_____

_____

_____

_____

_____

_____

_____

_____

_____

_____

_____

_____

_____

_____

Lesson 19: Thy Will Be Done

Many plans are in a man's mind, but it is the Lord's purpose for him that will stand.

(Proverbs 19:21)

Before Eric goes into court, Amber prays with him. How important is it for couples to pray together? Amber prays that God's will be done. What does this prayer mean? Are you able to accept God's will for your life?

_____

_____

_____

_____

_____

_____

_____

_____

_____

_____

_____

_____

_____

_____

_____

_____

_____

_____

_____

_____

_____

_____

_____

_____

Eric states that withholding a child from their father not only hurts the child and the father, but also impacts the extended family. Write down any thoughts you have about this statement.

_____

_____

_____

_____

_____

_____

_____

_____

_____

_____

_____

_____

_____

_____

_____

_____

_____

_____

Read Proverbs 19:21. Write down your thoughts and feelings about this verse and how it applies to your life.

_____

_____

_____

_____

_____

_____

_____

_____

_____

_____

_____

_____

_____

_____

_____

_____

_____

_____

_____

_____

_____

_____

Lesson 20: It's Time To Man-Up

When I was a child, I talked like a child, I thought like a child, I reasoned like a child; now that I have become a man, I am done with childish ways and have put them aside. (I Corinthians 13:11)

"It's OK to make mistakes and errors that hurt others when we are children; we don't know any better. But when we are adults, when we are men and are still hurting others despite the fact that we now know better, it is no longer acceptable. God is here and He is providing us the opportunity to love as He loves, but we are still being childish. Men, it's time to grow up. It's time to man-up. It's time to stop being selfish and self-centered. It's time to operate in the spirit of love. When someone acts rudely to you, treat them with kindness anyways. You're a grown man; you don't play tit-for-tat like a child anymore. When someone does you dirty, forgive them and forget about it. You're a man; you don't keep records of the wrong done against you like a child would. Grow up. If you want to call yourself a man, it's time to act like one. Man-up, Brothers, man-up."

Read I Corinthians 3:11. Based on the verse and the reading of lesson twenty:

Men: What childish ways do you need to put aside? How can you "man-up" in your marriage/relationship?

Women: God requires women to also put aside childish ways and behave like adults. What does this verse/lesson mean for you as a woman? What childish ways do you need to overcome?

_____

_____

_____

_____

_____

_____

_____

_____

_____

_____

_____

_____

_____

_____

_____

_____

_____

_____

_____

_____

_____

_____

_____

_____

_____

_____

_____

_____

_____

Often we hold on to childish behaviors, thoughts, and ways for a reason. Why have you held onto unproductive emotions and actions Write prayer below asking God to help you put aside every thought, feeling, behavior, or rationale that does not reflect wholeness in Him.

_____

_____

_____

_____

_____

_____

_____

_____

_____

_____

_____

_____

_____

_____

_____

_____

_____

_____

_____

_____

_____

_____

_____

_____

_____

_____

_____

_____

_____

Lesson 21: Exit, Stage Right

And I found that [of all sinful follies none has been so ruinous in seducing one away from God as idolatrous women] more bitter than death is the woman whose heart is snares and nets and whose hands are bands. Whoever pleases God shall escape from her, but the sinner shall be taken by her.

(Ecclesiastes 7:26)

Despite feeling reluctant, Eric agrees to meet with Jay at ESPN Zone. Why do you believe that he continues to fall for her antics? Why is it so difficult for him to keep his relationship professional with her or to decide to stop working with her? Is the monetary and/or career gain worth it?

_____
_____
_____
_____
_____
_____
_____
_____
_____

At the sports bar, Jay kisses Eric. Although he pushes her away, he does not tell his wife about the incident.

Men: Do you think this is a form of infidelity? Would you tell your wife/girlfriend? Why or why not?

Women: Do you think this is a form of infidelity? Would you want your husband/boyfriend to tell you?

_____

_____

_____

_____

_____

_____

_____

_____

_____

_____

_____

Read Ecclesiastes 7:26. Write down any thoughts or feelings you have about this verse.

_____

_____

_____

_____

_____

_____

_____

_____

_____

_____

_____

_____

_____

_____

Lesson 22: Once Was Blind But Now I See

For now we are looking in a mirror that gives only a dim (blurred) reflection [of reality as in a riddle or enigma], but then [when perfection comes] we shall see in reality and face to face! Now I know in part (imperfectly), but then I shall know and understand fully and clearly, even in the same manner as I have been fully and clearly known and understood [by God]. (I Corinthians 13:12)

"I used to wonder why God loved me so much that He would give His Son for me. Many Christians wonder the same thing. But one of the reasons we don't understand why is because we don't know who we really are. We cannot fully see ourselves the way He sees us. It's like a parent looking at his child and knowing all the wonderful things that the child possesses. That child may make mistakes and disappoint his father, but the father loves him anyway because the father sees and knows that child better than the child sees and knows himself. One day, that child will grow up and come into the full knowledge of all that he is, and then he will be able to understand his father's love."

Read I Corinthians 13:12 and lesson twenty-two in the Husband 101 book. Write down your thoughts and feelings about these verses and Martin's explanation of them. Are you able to see yourself for who God made you to be? How can you have a greater understanding of who you are?

_____

_____

_____

_____

_____

_____

_____

_____

_____

_____

_____

_____

_____

_____

_____

_____

_____

_____

Find the words to the song *Amazing Grace*. What do the lyrics mean to you (for your life)? How has God's grace restored your vision?

_____

_____

_____

_____

_____

_____

_____

_____

_____

_____

_____

_____

Lesson 23: What You Don't Know Can Hurt You

Pride goes before destruction, and a haughty spirit before a fall. (Proverbs 16:18)

Lena throws a curve ball in court by having her attorney reveal incriminating photographs of Eric with Jay. Do you think Eric deserved this blow-up in court? Do you believe that the truth always revealed in time?

_____

_____

_____

_____

_____

Eric is forced to tell his wife the truth about his business transactions with Jay.

Men: How hard is it to tell the truth even when you are wrong? How should your spouse/significant other respond to your confession? How would you respond if the situation were reversed?

Women: How would you respond if you were Amber? Are Eric's lies forgivable?

_____

_____

_____

_____

_____

_____

_____

_____

Were you surprised by Jay being involved in Lena's plan? Why do you think some women throw themselves at men who are unavailable?

_____

_____

_____

_____

_____

_____

_____

_____

_____

Read Proverbs 16:18. Write down your thoughts and feelings about this verse and how it applies to your life.

_____

_____

_____

_____

_____

_____

_____

_____

_____

_____

_____

_____

Lesson 24: The Greatest Gift Is Love

And so faith, hope, love abide [faith—conviction and belief respecting man's relation to God and divine things; hope—joyful and confident expectation of eternal salvation; love—true affection for God and man, growing out of God's love for us and in us], these three; but the greatest of these is love. (I Corinthians 13:13)

"There are a lot of things that we do for others, a lot of gifts that we give whether it's a physical present, a service, words, or some other form of giving. We often think we've done something major when we are able to give. We feel good about ourselves for our selflessness and thought, but, brothers, I tell you today that the greatest gift that anyone could ever receive is love. When people receive love, they receive God. Yes, receiving love is bringing people to God's salvation, but receiving love is also when people experience God's love through you. Every time you show your wife love, you are allowing her to feel the presence of God. Each time you share love with others, they get to know and see God through you. Loving people is powerful because God is revealed on this earth every time we choose to love. The next time you want to do something special for someone, love them; love them with God's love in you."

Read I Corinthians 13:13 and lesson twenty-four. Write down your thoughts and feelings about this verse and lesson.

_____

_____

_____

_____

_____

_____

_____

_____

Lesson 25: The Wages Of Sin Is Death

For the wages which sin pays is death, but the [bountiful] free gift of God is eternal life through (in union with) Jesus Christ our Lord. (Romans 6:23)

A tragedy occurs in lesson twenty-five. Who is to blame? Is it Amber's fault for continuing to work? Is it Eric's fault for stressing Amber out? What other factors should be considered?

_____

_____

_____

_____

_____

Eric states to Tisha, "Sometimes a woman should be with her female friends. There are some things that men just can't be there for you like you want." Do you agree or disagree? What did Eric mean by this statement?

_____

_____

_____

_____

_____

_____

_____

_____

_____

Read Romans 6:23. Write down your thoughts and feelings about this verse and how it relates to your life.

_____

_____

_____

_____

_____

_____

_____

_____

_____

_____

_____

_____

_____

_____

_____

_____

_____

_____

_____

_____

_____

_____

_____

_____

_____

Lesson 26: Do It For Heaven's Sake

Husbands, love your wives [be affectionate and sympathetic with them] and do not be harsh or bitter or resentful toward them. (Colossians 3:19)

"When we are living a life dedicated to God, everything we do must also be dedicated to Him. As we allow for God to abide in us and work through us, we become living sacrifices, vessels to be used by the Lord as He chooses. It is important that before we step into our roles as husbands, or any other role we may play, that we understand that we must first step into the role of worshiper. Worship is not just what you do on Sunday morning while the praise team is singing your favorite song. Worship is a lifestyle, a daily way to glorifying God in all that you do. Your life should be one of continuous worship. If so, loving your wife or any other command that He gives you will be as simple as breathing."

Colossians 3:17-19 and lesson twenty-six. Write down your thoughts and feelings about these verses and how this lesson applies to your life. How can you worship God with your life?

_____

_____

_____

_____

_____

_____

_____

_____

_____

_____

_____

_____

_____

_____

"The good thing about being broken by God is that once you surrender, there's no place to go but up." Do you agree or disagree with this statement. Why? Write any thoughts/feeling you have related to being broken by God.

_____

_____

_____

_____

_____

_____

_____

_____

_____

_____

_____

_____

_____

_____

_____

_____

_____

_____

_____

_____

_____

Lesson 27: No Man Is An Island

Where there is no counsel, purposes are frustrated, but with many counselors they are accomplished. (Proverbs 15:22)

Despite their marital issues, Amber supports Eric by attending court with him. How easy or hard is it for you to support your spouse/significant other when you are upset with them? How do you overcome your emotions to be there for your mate even during the toughest times?

_____

_____

_____

_____

_____

_____

_____

_____

Eric finds out that his wife intervened on his behalf to save the real estate deal. How do you feel about her intervention? What does her accomplishment say about utilizing the strengths of your mate?

_____

_____

_____

_____

Carl talks to Eric about marriage and that hard lessons learned. Write down your thoughts about this conversation.

_____

_____

_____

_____

_____

_____

_____

_____

_____

_____

Read Proverbs 15:22. What does this verse mean as it relates to your life?

_____

_____

_____

_____

_____

_____

_____

_____

_____

_____

_____

Lesson 28: Take The Lead With Love

However, let each man of you [without exception] love his wife as [being in a sense] his own self; and let the wife see that she respects and reverences her husband [that she notices him, regards him, honors him, prefers him, venerates, and esteems him; and that she defers to him, praises him, and loves and admires him exceedingly]. (Ephesians 5:33)

Men: During the last Husband 101 class, Martin returned the "Why do I love my wife?" list back to his students and asked them to adjust their reason if it has changed. Turn back in your workbook to lesson four and adjust your reason below if necessary. Has your reason changed? How so?

_____

_____

_____

_____

_____

_____

_____

_____

_____

_____

Women: Have your ideas or thoughts about love changed? If so, how?

_____

_____

_____

_____
_____
_____
_____
_____
_____
_____

"I am ending our time with this verse because I want you all to see the result of your loving. When you are obedient to God and you love your wife, wonderful change can occur in your marriage. Notice that the verse starts off requesting that men love their wives, but ends elaborating how women are to respect and reverence their husbands.

"My conclusion is this: When you take the lead with love, you set your family in order, and propel your wife to submit to you and respect you the way you desire her to as a man. Fellas, you no longer have to try to control your wife or force her to treat you like a king. All you have to do is love her with God's love in you; that's it. The Bible tells us that if we seek the Kingdom of God and His righteousness, His way of doing things, everything else will be added to us. It's time for us to step into our positions as men, putting order back into our homes, and it starts with love. When we set the example and lead with love, the various aspects of our lives will begin to line back up in their proper place, but we've got to make the first move. We've got to make the choice to love. Now that we understand this thing called love, let's embrace it, live in it, and lead the way with it."

Read the quote above as well as Ephesians 5:33. What conclusions can be drawn about the relationship between wives and husbands from this verse and quote? What is God requiring of men and women who are married? How does a man's obedience to his charge by God impact a woman's obedience to her charge?

_____
_____
_____
_____
_____
_____
_____

As the Husband 101 course ends, what have you learned about love and God's desire for marriage as it relates to love? How can you be more demonstrative of love in your marriage and/or relationships with others?

_____

_____

_____

_____

_____

_____

_____

_____

_____

_____

_____

_____

_____

_____

_____

_____

_____

_____

_____

_____

_____

_____

_____

Lesson 29: Falling Is Easy, Getting Up Is The Challenge

For a righteous man falls seven times and rises again, but the wicked are overthrown by calamity.

(Proverbs 24:16)

Eric and Amber meet with Martin and Lydia for a marital counseling session. Many emotions, beliefs, and perceptions are revealed during this meeting. Write down your thoughts about their session and any impact it had on your feelings about your own marriage or relationship.

_____

_____

_____

_____

_____

_____

_____

_____

_____

_____

_____

_____

_____

_____

Read Proverbs 24:16. Write down your thoughts and feelings about this verse.

_____

_____

_____

_____

_____

_____

_____

_____

_____

_____

_____

_____

_____

_____

_____

_____

_____

_____

_____

_____

_____

_____

_____

_____

_____

Lesson 30: No Place Like Home

He who finds a [true] wife finds a good thing and obtains favor from the Lord. (Proverbs 18:22)

Eric visits Lena and Gold after his fast to make amends with them. What do you think about these decisions? Would you have done the same? Why or why not?

_____

_____

_____

_____

_____

Eric meets with his parents and also makes some changes in the manner in which he deals with them. Do you agree or disagree with his choices regarding his mother and home church? How do you feel about his decision to forgive his father and welcome his half-sister into their family?

_____

_____

_____

_____

_____

Fast for five days, for five hours a day, and pray each hour during the fast (five times a day) as Martin directed Eric and Amber. At the end of the fast, write down your experience and what directives or revelations you have received from God about your marriage/relationship.

_____

_____

_____

_____

_____

_____

_____

_____

_____

_____

_____

_____

_____

_____

Read Proverbs 18:22. Write down your thoughts and feelings about this verse and its meaning.

_____

_____

_____

_____

_____

_____

_____

_____

Epilogue

Lesson 31: And Life Goes On

Life is in the way of righteousness (moral and spiritual rectitude in every area and relation), and in its pathway there is no death but immorality (perpetual, eternal life). (Proverbs 12:28)

Read Proverbs 12:28. Write down your thoughts and feelings about this verse. What is God speaking to you about right now about your marriage/relationship? What is God speaking to you right now about your life?

_____

_____

_____

_____

_____

_____

_____

_____

_____

_____

_____

_____

_____

_____

_____

_____

_____

_____

_____
_____
_____
_____
_____
_____
_____
_____
_____
_____
_____
_____
_____
_____
_____
_____
_____
_____
_____
_____
_____
_____
_____
_____

Notes

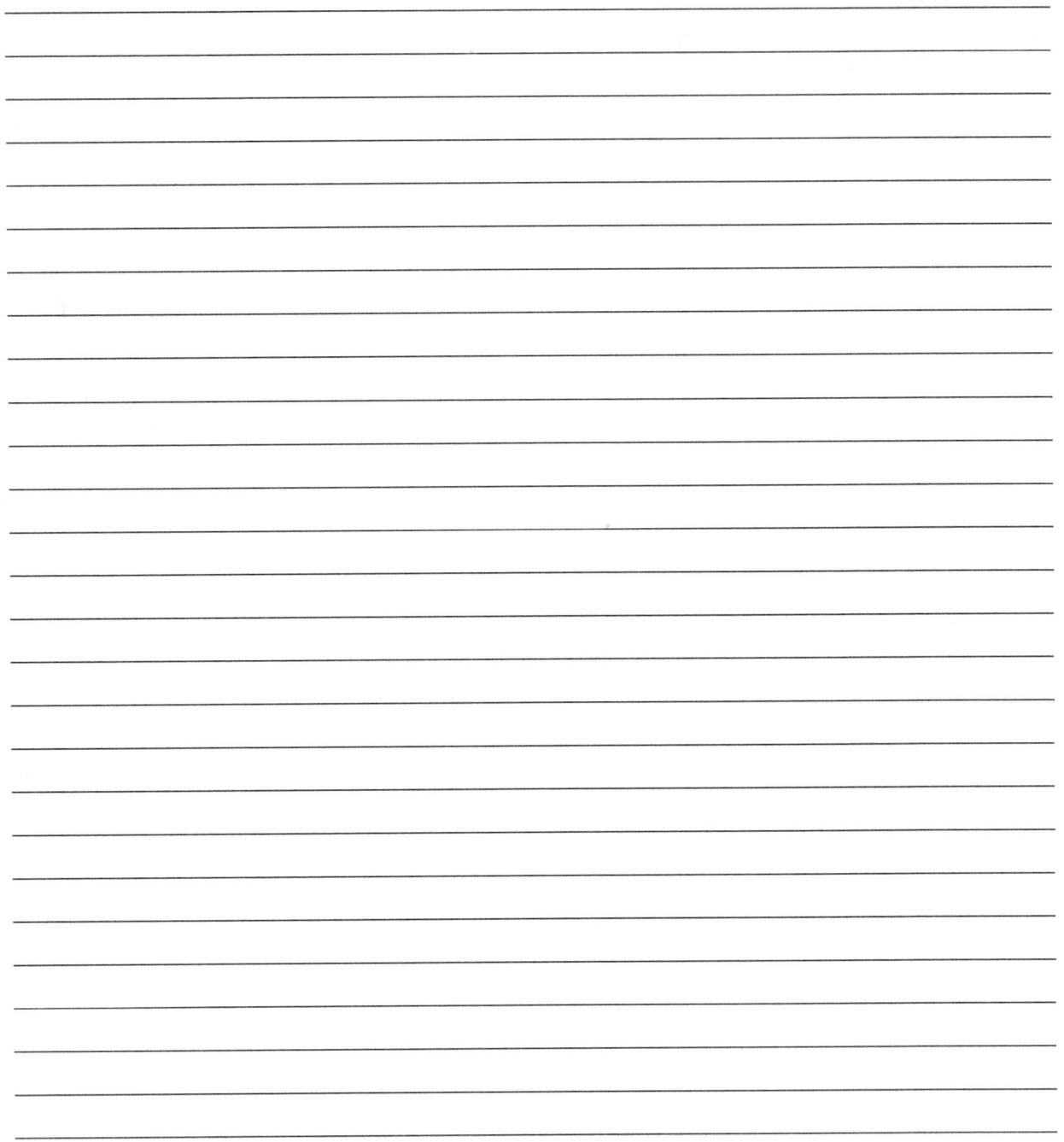

The saga continues October 2013!

Visit www.wife101.com for details.

A WIFE 101 SERIES NOVEL

Couples 101

A'ndrea J. Wilson

DIVINE GARDEN PRESS

Redeeming marriages & families one book at a time

UPCOMING RELEASES

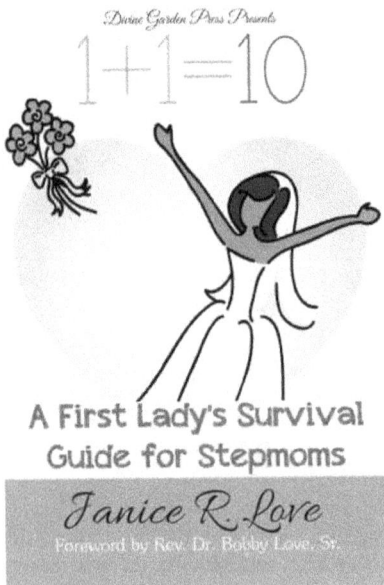

Divine Garden Press Presents
1+1=10
A First Lady's Survival Guide for Stepmoms
Janice R. Love
Foreword by Rev. Dr. Bobby Love, Sr.

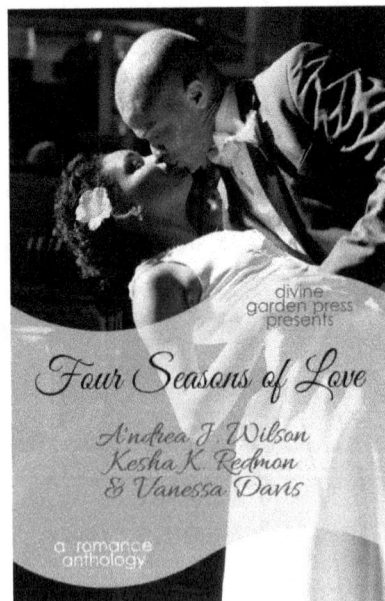

divine garden press presents
Four Seasons of Love
Andrea J. Wilson
Kesha K. Redmon
& Vanessa Davis
a romance anthology

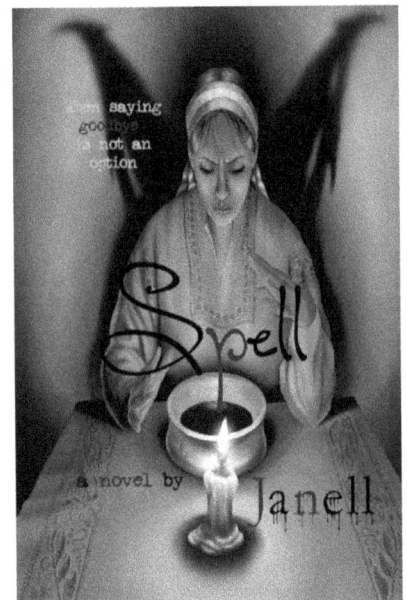

saying goodbye is not an option
Spell
a novel by Janell

WWW.DIVINEGARDENPRESS.COM

love it. review it. share it with a friend.

www.husband101.com

Husband 101

THE ANTICIPATED SEQUEL TO

WIFE 101

An Inspirational Novel by

ANDREA J. WILSON

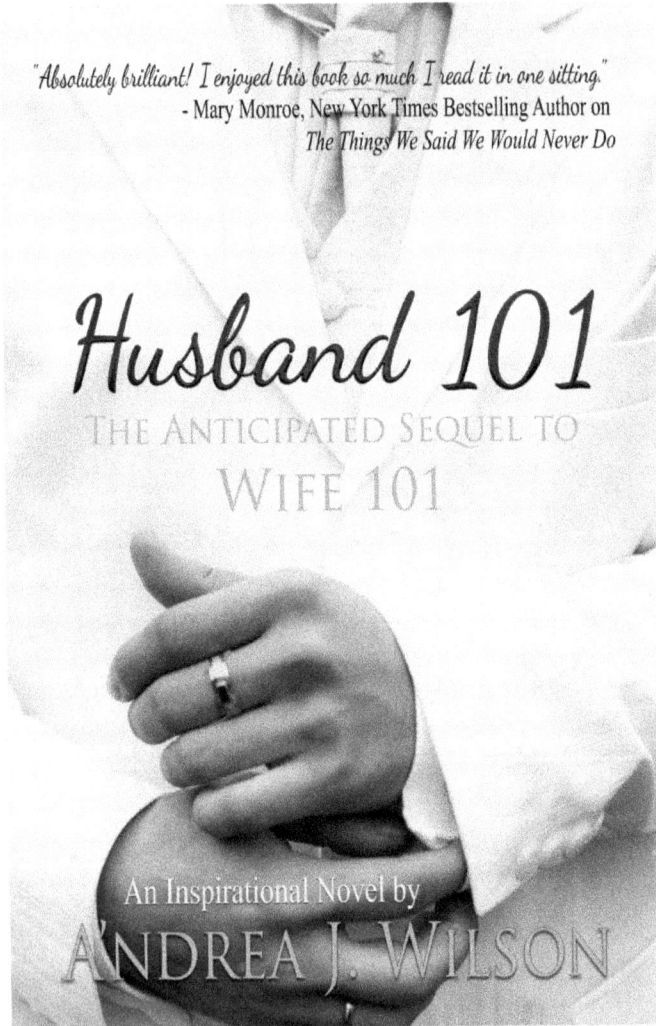

About the Author

A'ndrea J. Wilson, Ph.D. is the author of both fiction and nonfiction books, including the novels, *Wife 101* and *Husband 101*, and the devotional, *My Business His Way: Wisdom & Inspiration for Entrepreneurs*. She holds a Bachelor's of Science in Psychology, a Master's of Science in Counseling Psychology; Marriage and Family Therapy, and a Doctorate in Global Leadership; Educational Leadership. A'ndrea works as a college professor, as well as conducts workshops on a variety of personal and professional topics. Dr. Wilson is the Founder and President of Divine Garden Press, a publishing company that specializes in fiction and nonfiction books addressing marriage and family issues. She is a member of Zeta Phi Beta Sorority, Inc. and is frequently involved in community service activities. A native of Rochester, New York, she currently resides in Georgia. Please visit her online at www.andreawilsononline.com and www.wife101.com or email her at drajwilson@gmail.com.

Books by A'ndrea J. Wilson

Nonfiction

My Business His Way: Wisdom & Inspiration for Entrepreneurs

Kiss & Tell: Releasing Expectations

The Wife 101 Workbook

Fiction

Wife 101

Husband 101

The Things We Said We Would Never Do

Ready & Able Teens: Ebony's Bad Habit

Ready & ABLE Teens: Desiree Dishes the Dirt

Collaborations

"Grave" found in the Love Said Not So Anthology

He Loves Me, He Loves Me Not with Twilla Robinson-Booker

Four Seasons of Love Romance Anthology (Spring 2013)